"For our Dear friends

march 5, 1981

Byron, Mary Ann
Jamie, Jeremy

For your Ministry to
Us

"For our Dear friends

MAGNIFICENT AUSTRALIA

Jocelyn Burt

RIGBY

Contents

National Library of Australia
Cataloguing-in-Publication entry

Burt, Jocelyn
  Magnificent Australia
  ISBN 0 7270 0148 5
  1. Australia—description and travel
  I. Title.

919.404

RIGBY PUBLISHERS LIMITED • ADELAIDE
SYDNEY • MELBOURNE • BRISBANE
NEW YORK • LONDON
First published 1976
Reprinted 1978
Reprinted 1980
Copyright © 1976 by Jocelyn Burt
All rights reserved
Wholly designed and set up in Australia
Printed in Hong Kong

WARREN GORGE, FLINDERS RANGES

Great Dividing Range

Australia's backbone is its eastern highlands, known as the Great Dividing Range, and without it much of the country would be a useless wasteland. Extending from the top of Cape York Peninsula to western Victoria and reaching into Tasmania, the chain of ranges, plateaux and rolling hills that makes up the 'Great Divide' is a vital watershed for nearly half the continent, and gives birth to many rivers and streams that carry their precious, life-giving liquid far out to the plains. In places the Great Divide is up to 320 kilometres wide, sometimes embracing the coast or staying well inland.

The world over, beauty and mountains go together and the Great Divide is no exception. It holds in its terrain much of the country's loveliest scenery and a wealth of flora and wildlife. As to be expected from an area that has one end in the tropics and the other in a cool temperate zone, it contains a remarkable variety of climate and features; consequently there are many thrilling moods to experience. Wonderful contrasts are everywhere, in bold jagged bluffs and streamlined granite tors, in grand limestone caves, in bubbling streams, in thundering waterfalls and in placid lakes. When you wander through the balmy world of a lush rainforest in Queensland, where the sunlight filters softly through the green leaves and the air is warm and still, pause a moment and recall a bracing walk along a snow-lined road in the Victorian Alps, where the trees on the white slopes are burdened with snow, and your breath steams in the icy air.

At the top of Cape York Peninsula the steep ranges are wildly rugged. Further south near Cooktown, there lies the strange Black Mountain, a small part of the range completely covered in an extraordinary mass of black granite boulders that shine like gross beads of jet when the sun's rays are slanted in a certain direction. Except for an occasional straggling bush, the mountain is bare and the only living creatures that roam the slopes are rock wallabies and huge pythons. Once reaching the superb Atherton Tableland, lying between the Palmer River and the headwaters of the Burdekin River, the vegetation changes dramatically from light woodland and long grass to rainforest and dense jungle.

From the Tableland to the Queensland border, the highlands, still forested in many places, are mainly rolling hills and broad valleys with steep eastern slopes deeply folded into a myriad of minor hillocks. Nowhere is this more clearly seen than on the drive up to Eungella, inland from Mackay. In the lovely McPherson Ranges, not far from Brisbane, lies Mount Lamington, a national park renowned for its rich vegetation—in particular the splendid, ancient stands of Antarctic Beech. One of the best walks in the park is along the Border Track, following the edge of the very high plateau and commanding magnificent views over the New South Wales ranges.

South of the border stretches the vast New England plateau, the largest in the Great Divide, with an altitude of more than 915 metres (3000 feet). Perhaps the best known region in New South Wales is the Blue Mountains, lying near Sydney, and which, for many years after the foundation of the colony, presented a barrier to explorers seeking access to the country beyond. One of the great scenes of Australia is here at Katoomba, where three gigantic spires, known as the Three Sisters, rise in dignity from a precipitous cliff that juts out into the valley. The prevalent blue haze which gives the area its name is caused by particles of eucalypt oil that vaporise in the air and scatter blue lightrays.

After a broad depression around the vicinity of Goulburn, the Great Divide rises in wild splendour to its highest land mass, the Snowy Mountains, cradle of the country's highest mountain, Mount Kosciusko, 2229 metres (7314 feet). This region is known as the Australian Alps and dips well into the north-eastern corner of Victoria, remaining wild and inaccessible in many places. Some of the valleys on the western edge have been tamed, and in the beautiful and well-loved Ovens, Buffalo and Kiewa Valleys there is a mixture of softness and grandeur rarely seen to such an extent anywhere else in Australia. The Great Divide dominates more than half of Victoria. In the dwindling ranges of central Victoria lies some extremely picturesque scenery, as much of the land has been cleared for pastoral use and fortunately many trees have been left.

THREE SISTERS, KATOOMBA, NEW SOUTH WALES

MOUNT BOGONG, VICTORIA

Rising majestically from the floor of the Kiewa Valley to 1983 metres (6508 feet), Victoria's highest mountain is veiled in wreaths of lazy morning mist, soon to disappear with the wind. However, in winter, swirling clouds, grey and stubborn, seem often unwilling to display the glorious crown of snow that lies heavily on its peak. Mount Bogong dominates the little town of Mount Beauty, 354 kilometres north-east of Melbourne, and splendid views of the valley and the Southern Alps can be seen from the Tawonga Gap road that winds over the range between the Kiewa and Ovens Valleys.

Above:

LAKE EACHAM, NORTH QUEENSLAND

Lying 72 kilometres from Cairns, Lake Eacham nestles like a jewel in the lush rainforest of the Atherton Tableland. Its clear, still water fills the mouth of an old volcano and is one of several crater lakes that are on the Tableland, testifying that this area was once subjected to much volcanic activity. Except for a little rising and falling during the peak of the seasons, the lake's water level mostly remains constant at an average depth of 146 metres (480 feet). There are approximately six kilometres of walking tracks through this national park and one of the loveliest is around the rim of the lake, where the shaded path dips close to the cool water. It is so peaceful here that not even a passing breeze, intent on ruffling the glassy surface, can spoil the tranquillity of the scene. Fourteen kilometres away lies Lake Barrine, another lovely crater lake that is believed to be linked to Lake Eacham by an underground stream.

Bottom right:

DROVING CATTLE, NEW ENGLAND, NEW SOUTH WALES

The spacious and fertile plateau of New England, situated in northern New South Wales and containing the city of Armidale, is the largest highland area in Australia.

GOULBURN RIVER, VICTORIA

This scene is between Eildon and Thornton, near the weir. The river is at its loveliest in autumn, for in many places the banks are lined with willows that turn to shimmering lines of fluid gold for a few brief weeks of the season. The river has long been a popular site for holidaymakers, especially along the upper reaches where there are many beautiful picnic spots. Between November and April many a fisherman finds a restful nook from which to throw a line. He will be rewarded, too, because there is good fishing in this river. Rising on the wooded slopes of the southern ranges, the Goulburn River wanders over central Victoria for about 550 kilometres and collects the contributions of many creeks and streams as it makes its way to the Murray River. But by the time it enters the Murray near Echuca, the once broad and stately river has little water in its course because a number of dams, including the great Lake Eildon, have retained the bulk of its load for irrigation and because a network of channels ducts the water to the vast dry areas of north-western Victoria. The Eildon Dam alone holds more than six times the amount of water in Sydney Harbour. Now the Goulburn Valley can be supplied in times of drought, and the bulk of the floodwaters that for years tumbled down the river to spread over the plains has been checked to a large extent.

FROM HOTHAM HEIGHTS, VICTORIA

At Mount Hotham there are many magnificent views over the snow-covered Razorback Ridge to the ranges beyond that roll endlessly to the horizon. Mount Feathertop and Mount Hotham rise nobly behind the village of Harrietville at the end of the Ovens Valley, twenty-five kilometres from Bright. It is the high country around Mount Hotham that is known as Hotham Heights. The road up the mountain winds for many kilometres and in places trails over the top of a ridge where both sides suddenly fall away to alarming depths. In winter, when thick fog and snow-laden clouds often envelop the mountain and high winds sweep bitingly across the heights, this road can be perilous and vehicles frequently need snow chains to cope with mud and

ice. Snowfalls up to a metre deep can occur overnight; in fact, the machine known as a 'snow blower' can be busy for days clearing the road, mostly leaving huge banks of impacted snow on the roadsides — a sight guaranteed to delight all skiers. Every weekend in winter a steady line of cars makes its way to Mount Hotham, for the slopes offer good and challenging skiing. As well, there are many areas suitable for cross-country skiing. More and more people are exploring the wonderful white world of the high plains, where there is beauty in the glittering mounds of ice that have been fashioned to fantastic shapes by the wind; and where gums bend under their snowy burdens, while the windward side of every branch and twig is laced by blizzard-driven snow.

FALLS CREEK VILLAGE, VICTORIA
Situated 378 kilometres from Melbourne, and with ski slopes rising to 1800 metres (5905 feet), this resort offers some of the best skiing in Australia, and a number of important international ski races are held here each year. Accommodation in the village is good and there is easy access to lodges and slopes. Australia was one of the first countries in the world to make a sport out of skiing. It was introduced by some Scandinavian miners in the 1860s to pass away the time in the snowbound gold town of Kiandra, in New South Wales. Since then many Australians have discovered the exhilarating joy of jetting down a white slope where the only sound is the swishing of skis moving over firm snow that has been lightly powdered by a recent fall. The season officially starts at the Queen's Birthday holiday weekend in June and, in an average year, finishes early in October.

Top right:
TWEED VALLEY, NEW SOUTH WALES
Like lush green mats, cane fields spread over the beautiful Tweed Valley, where Murwillumbah is the commercial centre for the rich pastoral area.

Bottom right:
GLASSHOUSE MOUNTAINS, QUEENSLAND
One of the loveliest panoramas of the Glasshouse Mountains is from the Mary Cairncross Park, a delightful picnic ground set off the road near Monteville, high in the ranges behind Nambour. Good close-up views of the formations are best seen from the back roads of Caboolture and the little village of Glasshouse Mountains. These unique geological formations are plugs of ancient volcanoes, and their strange shapes standing out on the horizon reminded Captain Cook, in 1770, of the glass furnaces in Yorkshire.

ANTARCTIC BEECH TREE, MOUNT LAMINGTON, QUEENSLAND
This Methuselah of the forest, appearing incredibly ancient in its robe of green moss, is one of many that grow by a walking track extending far into the rainforest of Mount Lamington National Park. The age of the Antarctic Beech (*Nothofagus moorei*) is very much in question, and nobody has been able to say for sure just how old many of them are—the oldest figure suggested has reached 10 000 years. However, it is certain they are at least 1000 years old and forestry experts think the ones at Mount Lamington could be around 3000 years. They are believed to be relics of an ice age and now dying out—the ones in this national park are not regenerating from seeds, though shoots and suckers do grow from the base of an old stem.

GRAMPIANS, VICTORIA
This view is from the Boroka Lookout, on the Mount Difficult Road and overlooks Lake Bellfield and the village of Halls Gap in Fyans Valley. Lying 241 kilometres east of Melbourne and at the tail end of the Great Dividing Range, the Grampians is one of the country's richest floral regions, harbouring over 800 different plants, which is about one third of the State's whole indigenous flora. It is thought that the remarkable abundance of floral wealth here is due to the area providing a natural refuge for plants millions of years ago when the rest of the continent was undergoing marked geological upheavals. There are three main ranges. All have bold, precipitous bluffs on the eastern side and, to the west, slopes that fall away gently to merge with the valley's plain.

Above:

KOALAS, LONE PINE SANCTUARY, QUEENSLAND

Of the 500 odd species of Eucalyptus trees, the koala will eat only the leaves of about twelve, and since Europeans came to Australia the animal has been constantly threatened with extinction. It is places like the Lone Pine Sanctuary in Brisbane that have saved the koala from such a fate. The sanctuary's success in breeding them in captivity is a triumph for conservation, as surplus stock is constantly being released into parks and state forests. This lovable marsupial, known affectionately as a bear, is mainly nocturnal, so his favourite pastime during the day is sleeping in the fork of a tree. If he should have the misfortune to be disturbed, he will peer down with a charmingly vacant expression at the intruder for a few minutes before settling deeper into the branches.

Right:

MOUNT WARNING, NEW SOUTH WALES

A spectacular mountain dominating the Tweed Valley's landscape in the far north-east of the State, Mount Warning is the remnant of a volcanic plug. This winding road ends near the top of the mountain, but a well-graded path continues for four and a half kilometres from the car park to the summit. It is a lovely walk, especially through the lower part of the subtropical rainforest where there are some splendid trees, so tall and grand, and with buttressed roots rearing out of the ground like great ships' rudders. From the summit's tiny plateau which measures about thirty-five footsteps across and is surprisingly well shrubbed and grassy, the views are incredible. It really is like being on top of the world.

Left:

JOHNSTONE RIVER GORGE, NORTH QUEENSLAND

Situated in the Palmerston National Park, near Innisfail, this vantage point by the Palmerston Highway gives spectacular views over the gorge, where jungle-clad slopes drop steeply to the hurrying river, and where sunlight filters softly through the trees. Signposted walking paths in the park, cool under a luminous canopy of rainforest, lead to various waterfalls. One of the loveliest of these waterfalls is the Wallacha Falls (*see back cover*), which lies deep in the luxuriant growth of the jungle, yet only a short walk from the road. This park is on the Atherton Tableland, which averages about 760 metres (2500 feet) above sea level and, although in the tropics, has quite invigorating winters together with even more pleasant summers than the coastal areas.

Above:

ENDEAVOUR RIVER, COOKTOWN, NORTH QUEENSLAND

The broad mouth of the Endeavour River is best seen from Cooktown's Grassy Hill, which offers a magnificent panorama of the mountains and the wide meandering river, sprinkled with sand banks and edged thickly with mangrove swamps. Captain Cook made use of the hill as a surveying point in 1770, when he brought in his damaged ship *Endeavour* to the present site of Cooktown for repairs. The town lies on the eastern side of Cape York Peninsula, 340 kilometres from Cairns. For many years the road was notoriously bad but recently has been upgraded considerably. It is still rough, but any tourist who complains will get no sympathy from the locals, who think it is a fine road, and will say firmly, 'You should have seen it when it was bad!'

Tropical North

Australia's tropical north covers the splendid country stretching from Broome and the Kimberley in the far North-West of Western Australia, across Arnhem Land in the Northern Territory to the gigantic digit of land that is Queensland's Cape York Peninsula. It is a region of dramatic contrasts, where lonely sunburnt plains meet rugged mountains gouged deeply by raging and swollen rivers, where vast tracts of rough scrub and impenetrable forests give way to a confusion of mud flats laced by watercourses seeking the sea, and where swamps end in tangled mires of mangroves. It is home for an incalculable number of animals, birds and fish, and the traditional tribal land of many Aboriginal peoples, as given evidence by their legacies of the many wall paintings found in caves and rock shelters.

Much of this wildly beautiful land is inaccessible, and despite the impact of recent mining activities is still largely 'last frontier' country. Until the mineral boom gripped the Far North, the majority of Australians knew little about this remote region. But once mining roads opened up a few areas tourists were not far behind. Today roadwork continues, and beef roads are being upgraded as well as the mining routes.

The sight of so much bitumen stretching over the vast Kimberley plains would surely astonish, and delight, the region's first stout-hearted settlers, who went through incredible hardships to bring their huge mobs of cattle across the virgin wilderness of the top, from Queensland to the Kimberley in the 1880s. But how incredulous they would be if they could see the Ord Dam's vast expanse of water, lying among the stark, brilliantly coloured mountains like a pale sapphire, infinitely precious! Every year, after monsoonal rains had filled rivers and streams, the pioneers watched the Ord River wastefully pour out its abundance of life-giving water into the sea.

From Kununurra, near the Ord Dam, a wide ribbon of bitumen sweeps across the land and finishes at a uranium mining camp on the edge of the Arnhem Land Reserve, east of Darwin. Now that this area has opened up considerably, people can visit the many beauty spots and in the dry season, places such as the Jim Jim Waterhole, Yellow Water Lagoon and the East Alligator River Crossing are seldom free from campers.

Only a day need be spent in this region before the wild, almost primitive atmosphere begins to pervade the senses. This is heightened at night by the eerie noises that fill the bush. But no sound is quite as scary as the full-throated roar of the crocodile's mating call which reverberates around the swamps, drowning all other noises. However, any uneasiness of the night is soon eclipsed by the joys of the dawn, when the day is fresh and the sun as yet has little sting, and buffaloes, brumbies and kangaroos roam freely through the scrub littered with the North's incredible, fortress-like anthills.

Cape York Peninsula is gradually opening up too, although, unless enormously rich mineral deposits are discovered by the prospectors who are quietly probing the area, progress will continue to be slow. This is a good thing, as little of the peninsula is protected by national parks. Much of the land is formidably wild and inaccessible, particularly in the Far North, which is a world of jungle-clad ranges, innumerable rivers, lily-studded lagoons and sullen swamps where wildlife abounds. Though access is now easy to Cooktown, rough tracks leading to the bauxite mining town of Weipa and to the top of Cape York are only suitable for four-wheel drive vehicles. Fortunately the southern end of the peninsula is better served with national parks, and numerous waterfalls, lakes, caves and tracts of rainforest have been preserved.

There are only two seasons, the Dry and the Wet. For about eight months of the year during the Dry, little or no rain falls and the merciless sun cruelly bakes the earth. As the Dry ends, the humid days become unbearably hot. An air of expectancy and tenseness hangs over the land as mocking clouds build up only to disperse after sundown. Then about December, the Wet arrives with a vengeance and the stillness of the bush is shattered by violent storms; roads are turned into deep channels of mud and water and the country almost drowns in the deluge. Shortly, it is transformed into a world of vivid greens and the mantle of lush vegetation sparkles in freshness.

JIM JIM WATERHOLE, NORTHERN TERRITORY

Above:

NOURLANGIE ROCK, ARNHEM LAND, NORTHERN TERRITORY
Through scattered outcrops of rocks and large boulders, this track leads to Nourlangie Rock, which can be seen beyond the trees on the left. Rising to 265 metres (857 feet) in rugged splendour and forming part of the western escarpment of Arnhem Land, Nourlangie Rock is best known for the fine Aboriginal art galleries that are on rock walls and ceilings of caves in the area. Here and in other parts of Arnhem Land the X-ray style of art has reached a higher level of development than in any other part of Australia. There are also Aboriginal burial grounds around Nourlangie that fortunately have not been molested. Nourlangie Rock is one of several areas within the Aboriginal Reserve for which permits are not required, providing the visit is made in daylight hours only.

Right:

YELLOW WATER LAGOON SUNSET, NORTHERN TERRITORY
This lagoon is a backwater of the Jim Jim Creek, at the edge of the Arnhem Land Reserve. The Jim Jim is famous for its fishing, and the sizes of fish a man can catch here are those usually confined to dreams — or tall stories. The fish bite best just before and after the wet season, especially around sunrise and sunset. East of Darwin, many a sunset is like this one, with the sun expanding to an enormous disc and floating to the horizon in a film of haze. Tropical sunsets the world over are renowned for their loveliness, but the ones in this region receive even more help from a pall of smoke that can hang in the air from excessive burning off.

Left:
GEIKIE GORGE, WESTERN AUSTRALIA
Lying sixteen kilometres from the Kimberley settlement of Fitzroy Crossing, Geikie Gorge is easily accessible for the traveller passing through the far North-West. Geikie's story is a very old one, for over a countless number of centuries the thundering floodwaters of the Fitzroy River have cut through the remains of an ancient coral reef that formed about 350 million years ago. The waters smoothed the fossil cliffs to their present height of about twelve metres (40 feet). The limestone cliffs lining the canyon for many kilometres are fascinating; the two distinct features of them that remain in most people's minds are the brilliant colours which almost seem to have been splashed on with paint, and the incredible variety of markings, indentations and holes.

Above:
THE ORD DAM, WESTERN AUSTRALIA
This great dam traps the colossal flood waters of the Ord River, which is fed by cyclonic rains that fall only between December and March. At that time the serenity of the dry season's still, hot days changes to a violent mood of angry skies and tumultuous thunderstorms. The Ord Dam lies in the eastern Kimberleys, about 3220 kilometres from Perth and 885 kilometres from Darwin. The sprawling town of Kununurra, built in 1960, is the centre for the irrigation scheme. At Lake Argyle, where the Ord's storage waters cover an area around 910 square kilometres, there is a touch of civilization at the spacious tourist village, set high on a ridge that commands superb views over the dam and surrounding mountains. Wildlife abounds here now that there is permanent water.

23

VICTORIA RIVER CROSSING, NORTHERN TERRITORY

BOAB TREES, KIMBERLEY, WESTERN AUSTRALIA

The strange boab (or baobab) trees, with their swollen trunks and ungainly limbs, are a distinct feature of the Kimberley region and range over the sandy plains and low stony rises for about 160 kilometres inland. The young, relatively slender boabs certainly have more dignity than the old ones, whose boles become gnarled and distorted with age, often expanding to monstrous proportions. These grandfather boabs, squatting grumpily on the ground like grotesque characters out of tales of fantasy, are a constant source of amusement for the traveller. There are only two species of this tree, one in Africa, and the other in Australia (*Adansonia gregorii*), which is endemic to the North-West and capable of reaching many centuries in age. The trunks act as a storage reservoir for food and water, and the tree only bears leaves during the Wet. Consequently little shade is given from its bare, untidy limbs that resemble roots more than branches. The large nut-like fruit has dry pulp inside which tastes rather like cream of tartar and is said to be refreshing in humid weather. A popular name for the boab is a bottle tree, though these are not to be confused with the bottle-shaped trees in Queensland that belong to the Brachychiton genus. The most famous boab is the Prison Tree, situated seven kilometres out of Derby. The tree has an enormous girth with a hollow inside, and is reputed to have been used as an overnight cell for a group of prisoners before their being taken into the town.

KATHERINE GORGE, NORTHERN TERRITORY

This is the Grand Canyon, part of the beautiful second gorge of the national park, lying near the town of Katherine, 322 kilometres south of Darwin. For about twelve kilometres from the ranger's jetty, thirteen gorges shelter the Katherine River, and in a world of constantly changing colours and moving shadows, no scene remains the same for long. One of the loveliest times of day to see it is early morning, when the air is fresh and the reflections have not been disturbed by breezes. The only way to see the gorges is by boat, as in many places the sheer walls plunge deeply into the river. Each gorge is separated by shallow rapids, which visitors can walk around with ease to where a boat waits in the next gorge. For five gorges tourists travel in this fashion and, at the end of the fifth, after climbing a cliff and following a track along the top, one can look down on the sixth, seventh and eighth gorges, which offer a spectacular view from the cliff tops. In the fourth gorge, time is set aside for relaxation, swimming and a barbecue lunch, which is prepared on the sandy banks of a small beach tucked between great bastions of rock. The gorge provides a home for much wildlife, including the harmless freshwater Johnstone crocodile, and the tiny Fairy Martins, who flutter around their bottle-shaped nests like a cloud of butterflies. Every year they build nests in the caverns of the cliffs, and every wet season the raging river sweeps them away.

27

Left:

MILLAA MILLAA FALLS, NORTH QUEENSLAND

This delightful waterfall is situated in a picturesque clearing of lush tropical rainforest near the small town of Millaa Millaa, on the Atherton Tableland. Although it does not have the width, nor plunges to the great depths of some of Queensland's waterfalls, nonetheless the Millaa Millaa Falls is very beautiful. In its simplicity the fall of water resembles a bridal veil, as if held to the rock face by a clasp of ferns that allows it to tumble gently to the small pool below. Behind the falls, moisture-loving mosses and other plants cling to the damp wall. They are screened in a film of mist yet their greens are just visible to the naked eye.

Above:

ATHERTON TABLELAND, NORTH QUEENSLAND

Much of the Atherton Tableland was once covered with jungle like this, and the task of clearing it was indeed a mammoth one. Rainforests are still being cleared today for primary industry and it is fortunate that the Palmerston National Park protects a narrow strip of tropical bushland along the Palmerston Highway. The entire route from Innisfail to Millaa Millaa, which passes through this beautiful, lushly green rainforest, is one of the loveliest drives in Queensland. But not all activities on the Tableland have been peaceful, for during the second World War military forces were based in the area for jungle warfare training in these dense forests.

Above:
NEAR CAIRNS, NORTH QUEENSLAND
The splendid views along the Cook Highway, running from Cairns to Port Douglas in the north, are a never-ending delight for all travellers. It is hardly surprising that people flock to tropical North Queensland during the southern winter to enjoy the glorious scenery and warm sunny days.

Bottom right:
NORTH-WEST COASTLINE, WESTERN AUSTRALIA
Seen from the air, the rugged coastline of the far North-West appears even more torn and fragmented than a general map suggests. This section of the coast is near Cockatoo Island, which has one of Australia's richest deposits of iron ore. The only way to see the spectacle of this coastline is by air, as the country beyond is virtually inaccessible.

Top right:
CAPE YORK SUNRISE, NORTH QUEENSLAND
This is at Somerset, on the eastern tip of Cape York. Before Thursday Island took over the government headquarters for the Torres Strait in 1877, Somerset was the site for one of Britain's strangest plans for Australia. This inaccessible and remote spot on Cape York was to be a 'second Singapore' of the Empire, where commercial enterprises would flourish and a communications centre, together with a vital military and maritime post, would be established. It was all a glorious dream that was doomed to fail right from the start. What chance did it have in this hostile part of the country, where not only the Aboriginals rejected the settlers, but the soil too? However, for twelve years the new settlement struggled for its dreams—and survival—under the leadership of John Jardine, the first elected Resident Magistrate. The only reminder today of Somerset's past is two guns standing on a lonely hilltop that once guarded Jardine's palatial Government House.

The Centre

Many people will tell you that the soul of Australia lies somewhere in the ancient-looking and worn land of the continent's centre, where the stark and strangely beautiful landscapes reflect Dreamtime magic and the genesis of time. Where its spirit may be exactly does not matter, for everyone will find it in a different place. For some it may lie deep in a spectacular chasm afire in a midday glory of redness, or in a monolith of omnipotent splendour, or in a deep pool frothing with a mass of ancient cycads, or along a sandy track—as straight as the horizon to which it runs. Many people may even find it at nightfall in the profound silence that descends on the surrounding bush, when the diamond-studded canopy of the sky, displaying clouds of stars not seen in the cities, presses in close.

There is no specific boundary to Central Australia. It is an area that takes in the borders of four states and is approximately within an 800-kilometre radius from the town of Alice Springs, lying close to the geographical centre of the continent. The climate is an enigma, as normal weather patterns are more often than not disrupted by drought or excessive rains. In some areas the accepted annual rainfall is around 127 mm (5 in.) but years may pass between showers and, instead, the storms are of dust which sweep over the land with terrifying intensity. Then numerous wet seasons might well follow, trebling the usual rainfall and causing normally dry rivers and creeks to come down in flood. In a year of heavy rains, travellers venturing off the main roads must cope with bogs of mud instead of sand. Winters are refreshing with pleasant sunny days and cold, often frosty, nights; but in the summer, the temperature wastes no time in climbing into the forties centigrade.

Colour dominates Central Australia. No scene is the same in the morning or afternoon, sunrise or sunset, for the land responds wonderfully to the constant changing of directional light as the sun progresses across the sky. Even on the featureless plains of Sturt's Stony Desert, where vast seas of harsh gibbers stretch to the far, shimmering horizon, it is fascinating to see the play of light on the stones that change from deep, warm reds to hard, steel greys.

The terrain varies as much as the colours. From the gibbers in Sturt's Stony Desert, the plains turn to red sand, the flat monotony broken in places by sandhills that sometimes rise to great heights, and in the Simpson Desert, almost impassable ridges of red dunes swell from the plains like ocean waves, often bare, unwilling to give even a precarious foothold to plants. Inhospitable the dunes may be, but their marvellous symmetry in sculpted sand is one of the great spectacles of the Centre. In many inland areas there are plains studded with domes of sharp spinifex, and cheerless claypans that are sometimes thickly crusted with glittering salt, but mostly covered in flakes of dried earth which after rain turn into morasses of oozing mud.

Numerous ranges sprawl over the Centre, their crumpled folds clothed in a raiment of rubble which supports scant plant life, and are often topped by bold collars of craggy rock. The best known of all the ranges are the MacDonnell Ranges, a favourite with so many people because of its accessibility from Alice Springs and for the many spectacular gaps, gorges and chasms that cleave its hills. Some of the gaps are guarded by a pool of water which is usually icy cold, because the sun's rays visit only briefly the deeper recesses.

Much of the region's mystery and fascination lies in its strange monoliths, so bizarre in form and beauty that the visitor's sensations are mixed with awe and absolute astonishment. Ayers Rock, red monarch of the world's monoliths, rises 348 metres (1143 feet) dramatically above the surrounding plains, and no matter how familiar through photographs and paintings the traveller may be with it, he will nevertheless be amazed at its enormous magnitude. For this reason alone, it is worth experiencing the Rock. Thirty-two kilometres away to the west lie the Olgas, a circle of extraordinary domes, bare and red, that from a distance appear to be piled high upon each other, but are actually separated by narrow gullies. A much smaller monolith, yet remarkable in its unusual form, is Chambers Pillar, a spectacular white sandstone column over thirty metres (100 feet) high.

TWIN GHOST GUMS, NORTHERN TERRITORY

Two of the most famous ghost gums in Australia, these twins near Alice Springs stand gracefully by the road, with the Razorback Range—part of the MacDonnell Ranges—trailing into the distance. Many motorists and tourist buses pause here and capture the beauty of the trees on film or canvas before travelling on to Standley Chasm and Glen Helen Gorge. One of the finest moments to see this scene is at sunrise, when the first morning light touches the range and turns to crimson the great collar of rock topping its craggy slopes. The richness of colour depends on the atmospheric conditions of the morning. A winter dawn is particularly beautiful, for the sun's rays cut through the

crisp, frosty air and give a pristine brilliance to every blade of grass, flower, leaf and branch. Growing extensively throughout Central Australia, the ghost gum (*Eucalyptus papuana*) is one of the loveliest of all the eucalypts, with its white, often blemish-free bark that appears to fit the tree like a glove, wrinkling at the fork of the limbs in the manner of a soft fabric. Even by dusty roads they stand so pure and fresh, as if whitewashed before the dawn. The Aboriginal artists, Albert Namatjira and his son Oscar, reproduced the beauty of the ghost gum in their water colours, and one of Albert's most popular paintings includes these famous twins.

THE OLGAS AT SUNSET, NORTHERN TERRITORY

Thirty-two kilometres west of Ayers Rock lie the Olgas, a cluster of about thirty spectacular sandstone monoliths that over the ages have been fashioned by the elements into domes. The highest is Mount Olga, rising 546 metres (1791 feet) sheerly from the surrounding plain. Each dome is separated by a ravine, which supports a surprising abundance of plant life, sustained by moisture trapped in the gullies. The summits of some of the formations are accessible but difficult to climb — with the exception of the one known as Katajuta Lookout, situated to the right in the Valley of the Mice Women. Another popular walk, and a much easier one, is through the Valley of the Winds, so named for the strong winds that at times rush furiously through the narrow gully. The track twists through the ravine and takes the walker to a vantage point which overlooks the whole inner valley towards Katajuta Lookout and the incredible Buddha-like Wilu. It is a strange sensation walking in the Valley of the Winds as the rough conglomerate walls, studded with a million varieties of pebbles, tower to such awesome heights that they appear to lean alarmingly over everything in the ravine. Although Katajuta Lookout has by far the most spectacular views, the Valley of the Winds gives the visitor a better understanding of the character and grandeur of the Olgas.

Above:
PALM VALLEY, NORTHERN TERRITORY
The most accessible area of Palm Valley is situated on a tributary of the Finke River, 141 kilometres south-west of Alice Springs. Once in the valley, the vehicular track soon peters out. In order to see the splendid ancient cycads and palms, it is necessary to walk two or three kilometres, mostly over wide expanses of flat rock interspersed with stretches of sand and rock pools. Gradually the pools become more shaded by groves of graceful palms, and together with the surrounding rocky edges are usually mirrored beautifully in the still water. The lush vegetation that grows here is certainly at odds with the rest of the inland areas, but this small pocket is a remnant of the time long past when Central Australia was covered with tropical vegetation.

Right:
THE AMPHITHEATRE, NORTHERN TERRITORY
Guarding the entrance to Palm Valley is this superb natural amphitheatre of towering cliffs and rocky outcrops of many weird and wonderful shapes. One of the best known formations is Battleship Rock, which is relatively easy to climb — if you don't mind heights. The amphitheatre has always been of great significance to the Aboriginals, as various tribes used to meet here for corroborees. Many initiation ceremonies were held here too, and legend has it that tragedy fell on a certain tribe when one of the lubras dared watch her beloved son being initiated in a ceremony that was strictly for men only. The entire tribe was instantly turned to stone and this stretch of rock is said to be the woman's boy lying down during his initiation.

Above:

BIRDSVILLE TRACK WILDFLOWERS, SOUTH AUSTRALIA

Running from Marree to Birdsville, the Birdsville Track is one of the most infamous routes of the inland, with rolling sand dunes, seas of gibbers, claypans, and a few isolated homesteads along its 485 kilometres. Usually this area receives an annual rainfall of about 101 millimetres (4 in.); however, there are seasons when such large amounts of rain drench the country that it is swamped with water for days, sometimes weeks. Dry creeks flow for the first time in years, the new gravel-surfaced sections of the Track are punctuated with washaways and the rest turns into a horrible quagmire. The most treacherous part is around Goyders Lagoon, where the Diamantina River empties its waters into a maze of channels and spongy swamps, and after rain the road frequently disappears. When the land recovers and the hot sun shines once again, the desert is transformed into a paradise of wildflowers, and trees are reborn with fresh foliage.

Right:

AYERS ROCK, NORTHERN TERRITORY

The top picture shows the Rock at a stormy dawn. Clouds heavy in moisture blanket the sky, and the rising sun manages to slip through only for a brief moment to flare the Rock to rich red. The bottom picture is on a tranquil afternoon. This colossal piece of sandstone is the earth's greatest slab of exposed rock, with a circumference of nine and a half kilometres that rises to 348 metres (1143 feet) above the surrounding plain. The top of the Rock is fissured with deep gullies, lightning-scarred ridges and a countless number of rock holes that overflow after heavy rain, sending enormous volumes of water cascading over the sheer walls. For the white man Ayers Rock is one of the unique tourist attractions in the world; for the Aboriginal it is a ritual ground of sacred Dreamtime legends and myths, and the caves that perforate the base are richly decorated with their art.

Left:
COOPER CREEK, NEAR LAKE EYRE, SOUTH AUSTRALIA
Rarely does the Cooper empty its waters into Lake Eyre, and it is not the rain that falls in its mid- or lower-reaches that causes it to flow down this far, but abnormally heavy rains falling in south-west Queensland. Once it reaches the arid plains, the Cooper usually dries up, leaving a series of beautiful waterholes, many of them permanent. When it does come down in flood, its waters spread into a maze of shallow channels and billabongs, and for a time may cover the land for hundreds of kilometres — which is not an uncommon occurrence in the vicinity of Innamincka, situated near the border in South Australia.

Above:
DESERT DUNE, SOUTH AUSTRALIA
Fashioned by the wind, this dune lies at the edge of Sturt's Stony Desert, in the far north-east of South Australia. The desert is known for its vast seas of gibbers, where the stones vary in size from small pebbles to large jagged rocks. So desolate is the gibber country that, even in good years of rain, plant life struggles to grow. The stony plains are broken in places by areas of canegrass and spinifex, and ridges of red dunes. After good rains, the bases of the dunes are often garlanded with a profusion of wildflowers, but it is at sunrise and sunset that they are at their loveliest, when the first and last rays of the sun turn them into hills of blood-red splendour.

41

Top left:

HEAVITREE GAP, NORTHERN TERRITORY

Through this gap, which is the gateway to Alice Springs, passes a river, road, railway and telegraph line. After heavy rains it is not unusual for the Todd River to demand all the space.

Bottom left:

THE DEVIL'S MARBLES, NORTHERN TERRITORY

Situated 400 kilometres north of Alice Springs, these extraordinary rocks lie scattered for many kilometres on both sides of the Darwin road, south of Tennant Creek. They come in many shapes and sizes, some standing alone, others piled on top of each other in such an astonishing manner that one feels there must be a more imaginative reason for their formation than the scientific explanation. The geologists tell us that due to intense weathering and sharp changes of temperatures, the outer layers of granite flaked away leaving the rocks rounded in form. The Aboriginal legend is much more interesting; it says the Marbles are the eggs of the rainbow serpent, a Dreamtime being linked with the source of all life.

Above:

BLANCHE CUP, SOUTH AUSTRALIA

Like a crater on the crest of a miniature volcano, this circular pool tops a small hill similar to the larger one in the distance. Blanche Cup is one of many strange formations known as mound springs that lie in groups between Marree and William Creek, in an area so desolate that at dusk it could well be a lunar landscape. With the exception of two—Blanche Cup and the Bubbler—all are virtually extinct. Situated around the south-western periphery of the Great Artesian Basin, the mounds were formed by drifting sand and artesian springs depositing heavy mineral salts as the water evaporated. As the mounds built up over the ages, water collected at the top, spilling over the side in one or more spots, before eventually drying up. Their sizes vary tremendously; some of the older ones rise to about 40 metres (130 feet) from the plain, others may only be about five metres (16 feet) high. The Bubbler, lying about one kilometre north-east of Blanche Cup, is a delightful entertainer, for at intervals of about ten minutes the placid pool suddenly begins to swirl in a frenzied manner and a growing bubble of mud struggles to escape. It may burst with great aplomb, or just disappear slowly as the water settles down. Blanche Cup is restless, too, and at irregular intervals thousands of tiny bubbles rise to the surface; the pond resembles a pot of water just starting to simmer. Blanche Cup lies close to the road, near Coward Springs.

43

KINGS CANYON, NORTHERN TERRITORY

Lying in the George Gill Range, 370 kilometres south-west of Alice Springs, this incredible canyon with its towering wall 182 metres (600 feet) from the valley floor, is one of the Centre's most spectacular and thrilling sights. The wall here, seen from the head of the canyon, is so smoothly sheer that it appears to have been sliced by a colossal knife. To get to the head of the canyon, it is necessary to walk up to the plateau and along it for about a kilometre, and although the walk is easy enough, for a first visit it is wise to join a guided tour (which is an exceptionally good one) as it is easy to get lost. The plateau itself is unique, and consists of a maze of small valleys topped by domed ridges which have a rock texture so old-looking that the overall effect is one of a ruined city. Tucked behind the head of the canyon is a narrow cleft known as the Garden of Eden, which is full of lush and very beautiful vegetation, including many cycad palms that cluster around perfectly still pools of limpid water. In the main valley there are more cycads growing among enormous chunky boulders that broke away from the north wall in ages past. It is believed that the last rock fall was about 2000 years ago; if there had been one in recent times the ancient cycads would no doubt have been damaged.

44

CHAMBERS PILLAR, NORTHERN TERRITORY

This solitary monolith, which millions of years ago formed part of a mountain ridge, stands at the edge of the Simpson Desert, about 200 kilometres south of Alice Springs. From a massive pedestal, covered with loose, rough stones of all sizes, the fluted column of sandstone, chafed and worn by the elements, rears thirty metres (100 feet) above the plains of red sand, dwarfing everything in its proximity. From the plains, a human being appears a mere speck when standing at the base of the pillar, on the hill. Chambers Pillar was discovered by John McDouall Stuart in 1860, and became a landmark for explorers and surveyors, many of whom left their names on its surface. To see such a tor standing keenly against the horizon of a vast wilderness must have been a welcoming sight to the explorers, and if they drew near at sunset, when its red cap changes to rich crimson, the pillar would have appeared like a flaming beacon against the evening sky. The explorer Ernest Giles poetically described it as a 'vast monument in its loneliness and grandeur, mystic and wonderful'. The modern-day visitor, if he has had any associations with shipping, will declare that it bears a remarkable resemblance to the conning tower of a submarine.

To the South-East

Nature lovers in Australia's south-eastern regions are indeed fortunate, as there are many places of scenic beauty and areas rich in flora and birdlife that lie close to the cities and towns. This is particularly so in Victoria, and probably nowhere else in Australia is there such a degree of weekend activities of camping and day-tripping as there is in that state. More and more people are discovering its manifold joys.

In the cooler areas of Victoria and New South Wales the country takes on many different forms of beauty during the four distinct seasons. Spring has the sweet-smelling wattles and delicate blossoms, while summer gives the land much warmer colours than any other time of the year. April and May are delightful months when the pageant of autumn displays its splendour in trees, glowing in reds and golds, that line the rivers, roads and even the towns' streets. The fallen leaves pattern the ground as they wait to be blown away by the bitter winds of winter. In the Alps, after the winter mantle of snow has melted, the high plains and the mountain slopes are covered in a profusion of alpine wildflowers, and in the Kosciusko National Park the floral display is indeed a wonderful sight.

Blanketed in snow for at least six months of the year, the high slopes of the Snowy Mountains give birth to many rivers, including one of Australia's greatest, the Murray River. As well as playing an important role in feeding water through irrigation channels to New South Wales, to Victoria's Mallee and Wimmera, and to much of South Australia, the Murray River has some wonderful scenery along its banks, lined as they are with gum trees, splendid cliffs and backwater lagoons.

Some interesting and spectacular features of the South-East are the remnants of volcanic activity, extending from Victoria's Western District into South Australia. Situated near Hamilton, the crater lake of Mount Eccles, with its shady trees and brilliantly green water, is totally different from the dramatic grandeur of Tower Hill's extensive crater lake. Near Warrnambool, the Tower Hill lake harbours islands that were once cones of ash, and lies among grassy folded hills, so stark at dawn and dusk. A splendid extinct volcano in the far corner of South Australia is Mount Gambier. It is topped by four beautiful crater lakes, one of them the phenomenal Blue Lake, which every

November mysteriously changes overnight from a dreary grey colour to an incredible vivid blue.

Not all the beauty lies above ground in the Mount Gambier district, for the region is riddled with subterranean limestone caves and tunnels, formed by water erosion in ages long past. Several of the caves with superb stalagmite and stalagtite formations have been opened to the public. Many of the caves have openings in the ground, of which about 200 have been recorded, and the eighty odd that are filled with water are known as sink holes. One of the best known of these is Piccaninny Ponds. These holes have become extremely popular with scuba divers, for their beauty is unlike anything else known, and those near Mount Gambier are unique because of their depth. Many of them have glorious underwater gardens filled with an abundance of plant life that floats serenely in the crystal-clear water. But it is the fantastic caverns, some enormous and opening out at the end of tunnels, that mostly lure the divers. Here is a weird and unearthly world where the water is so clear that a torch beam could be shining through air as it lights up incredible rock formations many metres away. The diver feels as though he is suspended in space, infinitesimal in such a vast grotto.

In South Australia some of the finest scenery lies in the State's largest system of ranges. These start with the Mount Lofty Range, which gently rolls along the eastern edge of Adelaide, and eventually run into the Flinders Ranges north of Port Pirie. Some of the most picturesque scenery of the southern part is in the Adelaide Hills, where superb gums, immortalised by the artist Hans Heysen, grace the camel-coloured slopes that in winter turn a rich green. Much further north, past Quorn, the indomitable Flinders Ranges present magnificent scenery that becomes wilder and more grand as the mountains push north into the arid regions. There are rugged gorges which have a cathedral-like atmosphere in their spaciousness, and ravines with cool and still waterholes that cling like limpets to the steep rocky walls. From the splendid, craggy ridgetops of Arkaroola, there are marvellous panoramas of rocky valleys, separated by massive mountain walls and narrow spurs. These finally and sharply give way to the endless plains, where the glittering line of Lake Frome's bed of salt lines the horizon.

Top left:
TOWER HILL GAME RESERVE, VICTORIA
Lying near Warrnambool, in the Western District, this extinct volcano is estimated to have been active only about 5000 years ago, and at that time, huge quantities of ash were blown out to cover a large area of surrounding countryside.

Bottom left:
WATTLE, NEAR WANGARATTA, VICTORIA
The national floral emblem of Australia, and a herald of spring, the yellow-gold wattles brighten the bushland and fill the air with a perfume that is distinct and sweet. As enjoyable as the pleasant aroma of the bloom is in the bush, once indoors, it can be quite overpowering; and like so many Australian native flowers, the wattle dies fairly quickly after being picked. The largest genus in the flora of Australia, the wattle (*Acacia*) is well distributed throughout the South-East, extending into Queensland and the arid areas of the inland. It has over 600 species, which is more than half the total number occurring in the world. In Europe the acacia is known as Mimosa but, to the horror of British botanists, the early Australian settlers called it a wattle tree, as its long, pliant twigs were ideal for making 'wattle and daub' huts. 'Wattle' is a term used for the thin branches in general that held together the walls of mud.

Above:
STRZELECKI RANGES, VICTORIA
Winding along the crests of the ranges for about 165 kilometres in South Gippsland, the Grand Ridge Road has many views of steep, tightly-folded hills cleared for farming, of mountain ranges, of lovely woodlands and of dense forests. Here nature displays every shade of green imaginable, appearing richer on damp, misty days.

49

KANGAROOS, SOUTH AUSTRALIA

This almost wholly herbivorous marsupial belongs to the Macropodidae family — appropriately meaning 'great footed' — of which there are about fifty species, including the wallabies, rat and tree kangaroos. To see a mob of large kangaroos bounding gracefully over the countryside, their sturdy tails propelling each swift leap, is indeed a thrilling sight. One leap can easily extend to eight metres and, when running in fear, the big ones may jump over a fence as high as two-and-a-half metres. As for speed, the kangaroo has been known to keep pace on flat ground with a car travelling at fifty kilometres an hour. If the animals are given a hard chase, their young are freed from the pouches; however, it is thought that this action is not so much the mother acting to save the baby 'joey' as a case of the pouch's muscles becoming tired. But the kangaroo's most remarkable feature is its birth. The newborn baby, which is virtually still an embryo and only a couple of centimetres long, crawls through the fur of the mother's belly to the inside of the pouch without any assistance whatsoever, and once inside searches the vast, furry area for the teat. To the despair of farmers, these animals are prolific breeders, as the female may have one growing in the womb, one in the pouch fastened on to a nipple, and a bigger one outside the pouch yet sucking.

LITTLE DESERT, VICTORIA

In spring the mallee scrub of the Little Desert is transformed into a superb garden wilderness and nowhere is the floral display as splendid as around the waterholes of its western end, near Kaniva. Above is Gartner's Camp waterhole, where the pink calytrix and golden acacia spread for hundreds of square metres away from the pool. In December a small forest of callistemons edging a portion of this waterhole is splashed with vivid red bottlebrush blooms that bedeck the trees like fat Christmas candles. Other waterholes and swamps are fringed with dainty yellow villarsias and fragile dichotomas—their mauve, fairy-like skirts fluttering in the gentlest of breezes. Giant river red gums dwarf the stringybarks; splendid stands of yellow gums tower over the scrub and give way to thick forests of banksias and seas of snowy white tea trees. Lying between Dimboola and the South Australian border, this unusual area called a desert—which it is not—shelters more than 650 species of plants, including an abundance of orchids, and has over 200 birds plus a wide variety of reptiles and animals. This is the home of the industrious and unique mallee fowl, or lowan, the only one of twelve mound-building birds in the world to inhabit an arid area. Because of the fluctuation of inland temperatures, the lowan has a much harder job in controlling incubation of its eggs than its cousins who inhabit the more evenly-temperatured tropical and subtropical areas.

51

Left:

NEAR NARRANDERA, NEW SOUTH WALES

It is not uncommon for travellers to come upon a stock muster when passing through the New South Wales Riverina, and the sight of a large mob of sheep, together with the stately gum trees that punctuate the plains of golden grass, help to form much of the character of the Australian rural scene. Situated on the Murrumbidgee, 586 kilometres south-west of Sydney, Narrandera is surrounded by broad, irrigation-fed plains that rise to 176 metres (576 feet) above sea level. It is one of the oldest towns in the Riverina, is an important road-and-rail junction, and a centre for a rich primary-producing area. The town's name is an Aboriginal word for a place of many lizards.

Above:

MURRAY RIVER, SOUTH AUSTRALIA

At Nildottie, a small settlement lying about 80 kilometres upstream from Murray Bridge, the Murray River spreads out into numerous lagoons and billabongs. From the cliff tops here, there are some wonderful panoramas. Between Swan Reach and Mannum lie some of the river's finest scenery, much of it sheltered by splendid, colourful cliffs of limestone believed to be between twelve million and twenty-six million years old, as many enlightening fossils of marine origin have been found there. There is beauty, too, in the broad and serene backwaters that mirror the trees and grasses. Here bird life is prolific and fortunately it is protected in many areas declared as sanctuaries. As this region is relatively close to Adelaide, colonies of holiday shacks line the banks near small towns.

Above:
KOOKABURRA
The kookaburra's ringing laugh, so full of hilarity and glee, is the most welcoming sound for an Australian returning from abroad. It is not even necessary to go into the bush to hear it, for the bird inhabits quite a few suburban areas of the big cities. Its name is one of the forty-odd recorded Aboriginal names given to the bird. Originally called the laughing jackass by the early settlers, the kookaburra is the largest of Australia's ten species of kingfishers, which are noted for their strong beaks and diets of insects, fish and small reptiles. The kookaburra may even swallow a young snake, digesting the lower portion while the rest hangs from its beak. Its true home is eastern Australia, but around the turn of the century it was introduced to Western Australia, and later to Tasmania, and easily became established in both areas. Its favourite nesting place is in the hole of a tree.

Right:
BLUE LAKE, MOUNT GAMBIER, SOUTH AUSTRALIA
A lovely remnant of volcanic activity in the South-East is this crater lake, famous for its dramatic overnight change in colour from grey to brilliant blue every November. However, the change back to its cheerless winter colour takes place gradually between March and June. Nobody knows why this happens, for the other three crater lakes that lie nearby remain constant in colour. All four lakes act as natural basins and have water continuously seeping into them through porous limestone. Lying 450 kilometres from Adelaide in the far south-eastern corner of the State, the city of Mount Gambier sprawls beside one of a group of extinct volcanoes that are in the district. Most of the mountain, which rises abruptly from the plains to a height of 190 metres (623 feet) is reserved for forestry and tourist purposes and there is a lovely scenic drive around the lake.

Above:

PICHI RICHI PASS, FLINDERS RANGES, SOUTH AUSTRALIA

This delightful gap, lying between Port Augusta and Quorn, is a gateway to the magnificent Flinders Ranges. Dominating the steep, main section of the pass, is the craggy Devil's Peak. An old picturesque railway bridge spans the road and is one of the few reminders of the days when trains used to pass through Pichi Richi on their way to Alice Springs. The mass of soft, mauve wildflowers carpeting the pass—and which cover many other parts of the Flinders—is the weed Salvation Jane, a plant welcomed in the arid areas as it is good fodder for stock. But in other states, this herb from the Mediterranean, which spread from one man's garden near Albury in New South Wales, is considered to be an absolute menace to the land.

Right:

BRACHINA GORGE, FLINDERS RANGES, SOUTH AUSTRALIA

This long and wildly-beautiful gorge that once had many bullock wagons pass by its towering cliffs lies at the foot of the Aroona Valley in the Flinders Ranges. Except when in spate, Brachina Creek trickles quietly through the gorge, sometimes harbouring water-loving plants if the flow of water is very slow, and filling numerous waterholes which at dawn and dusk reflect the rich colours of the rocks. Some of the rocks at the western end of the gorge contain fossils believed to be around 250 millions years old. In fact, when water is thrown over them, the fossil patterns show up dramatically. Brachina Gorge and Aroona Valley are favourites with painters, photographers and nature enthusiasts. It is hardly surprising that an early traveller once stated that, 'the loveliest twenty miles in Australia lies between Wilpena and Aroona'.

The West

Western Australia totals one third of the continent, much of it arid and uninhabited. Often its vastness is not fully appreciated until a motoring trip is undertaken from one end to the other, and then only if the motorist has unlimited time.

One area in the North-West that deserves to be given ample time is the Hamersley Range, in the Pilbara region. This massive range looks promising long before reaching the town of Wittenoom. In the late afternoon, it is a wonderful sight that looks like a great mountain rising proudly over the plains and appearing to be swathed in folds of soft velvet, all hues of mauve and purple. But once on the range's plateau the scene changes sharply, for the spinifex-studded plain is agape with deep, spectacular gorges that reveal terraced walls of rich chocolate, rusty browns and reds. Its unbelievably vivid colours are accentuated by the golden bloom of a beefwood or a lush green fern growing by a pool lying deep in a gorge. Looking down at the frighteningly sheer walls that in some instances plummet to 150 metres (500 feet) is indeed an awesome sight.

Probably the strangest scene in Australia is the Pinnacles Desert, lying north of Perth in the Nambung National Park, where erosion has exposed limestone spires of all shapes and sizes. In many places the sand is held together by a unique crust that appears to be tiny petrified roots only a few centimetres long, some lying on the ground, others valiantly erect, like minute icicles of sand. They are so fragile that at the lightest touch they will disintegrate, leaving the sand free underneath to drift according to the whim of the wind. A one-way track loops through the desert to enable visitors to see the pinnacles without causing undue destruction of the precious crust. The park's best protection is the road going to it from Cervantes, for the last section is full of rocks so large that even driving a car of good clearance is like navigating a boat through a wicked coral reef.

Another interesting national park is Kalbarri, situated on the coast about 640 kilometres north of Perth. Its grand coastline is indented with gorges, unusual rock formations and brilliantly coloured cliffs. The park's main feature is the Murchison River Gorge. For more than eighty kilometres the meandering Murchison River has incised a deep and wonderful canyon through layered sandstone, topped by sandy plains covered with interesting flora. There are a number of lookouts along the cliffs, but the one situated over the Loop area shows best how the river has shaped the gorge to its twisting course.

In the south-west corner, there are some interesting coastline, lovely pasture lands, limestone caves and timber forests. Around Pemberton and Walpole is the kingdom of the giant trees, the karri, jarrah and tinglewoods, and it is well worth while taking at least one of the scenic drives through these majestic forests. A famous karri is the Gloucester Tree, a fire lookout, which has a small hut perched like a pin head at the top of its 65 metres (212 feet) of trunk. Visitors are permitted to have the questionable pleasure of climbing this 300-year-old tree. Many people declare it a feat to reach the top and return safely—but surely the construction of the ladder that winds around the trunk, and the installation of the hut at the top, is a greater one!

The West's outstanding feature is surely her wildflowers. Spread over a wide variety of terrain, more than 7000 species are found, of which at least 4000 are endemic. But it is the utter profusion in which they grow that is so wonderful. Natural scrubland and plains are transformed into wild gardens blazing with colour, their floral wealth spilling out to the very edges of the road, and filling the air with strong scents of honey. Even in the rural areas, every vestige of land that has escaped being cultivated is likely to display a mass of flowers. In just a few square metres an astonishing variety of plants can be found, and the flowers themselves seem more brilliantly coloured and diverse in form than those in the eastern states. The strangest of all is the splendid kangaroo paw, the State's floral emblem. As in other parts of Australia common names for the flowers can be fun, and the West has its share of delightful ones, for there are pixie mops and redcoats, snottygobbles and toothbrushes, snake bushes and honeypots. Some of the State's favourite places for wildflowers are Kalbarri and the Murchison River, Yanchep and around Geraldton; and to the south-west, Lake Grace, Albany, Walpole and the Stirling Range.

GORDON OXER LOOKOUT, HAMERSLEY RANGE

Above:

STIRLING RANGE, WESTERN AUSTRALIA

Adorned with a profusion of wildflowers, this roadside scene is typical of the Stirling Range during the spring months. Nature lovers are almost overwhelmed by the riot of colour and the wide variety of species—in all about 600 of which fifty are peculiar to the area—that grow in this impressive but rather sombre mountain range. Lying about ninety kilometres north of Albany in the south-west of the state, and rearing abruptly over the wide plains, the Stirling Range is an important national park with a number of challenging hiking tracks. Of the many rugged and stony-faced peaks, Bluff Knoll is the highest, rising to 1109 metres (3638 feet). In winter, its shroud of mist may lift briefly to reveal a small cap of snow.

Right:

WAVE ROCK, WESTERN AUSTRALIA

Appearing as a wave frozen in stone, this extraordinary solid granite formation has been weathered and worn relentlessly by nature over a period of possibly 2700 million years. Wave Rock, as it is aptly called, lies just out of Hyden, in the South-West's wheat belt, 350 kilometres east of Perth. Its wall, ribboned with colours that have come from chemical deposits washed out of the rock by rain, rises to about 15 metres (50 feet) over the rocky floor. Allow more than a few minutes to explore this unique feature, for you will then experience the odd sensation that at any moment the rock will actually break, just as a wave breaks in the surf. There is another strange formation near Wave Rock known as the Hippo's Yawn, which looks remarkably like the gaping mouth of that animal.

Left:

MILLSTREAM, WESTERN AUSTRALIA

Lying off the Roebourne–Wittenoom road, Millstream's lovely deep pool wells from a natural spring and flows into the Fortescue River. Rimmed by lush vegetation and covered in parts by water-lilies, this oasis succours much wildlife, including a large colony of flying foxes. It is also a refuge for the rare and ancient palm, *Livistona alfredii*, which only grows in a vicinity of twenty-nine kilometres along the banks of the Fortescue River. The palm's nearest relative is in Central Australia's Palm Valley, and both plants are thought to be remnants of the period when inland areas had a tropical climate. More and more tourists are calling into Millstream, as this treasure of the north is in great danger of being flooded by a proposed dam.

Above:

PINNACLES DESERT, WESTERN AUSTRALIA

The strange Pinnacles Desert, where erosion has exposed limestone spires of many weird forms, lies on the coast 208 kilometres north of Perth. The pinnacles are there in thousands, covering many hectares of golden sands, and when seen from the top of a ridge, the view is that of a lost world. It is thought that each pinnacle extends deep into the ground, showing only its tip. The spires resemble a group in the Sahara that rise to heights of 580 metres (around 2000 feet). This small desert seems quite alien to the character of Australia; in fact, it seems more like a scene from the pages of the Bible. One almost expects a zealous prophet with long hair and burning eyes to leap out from behind one of the tall pillars.

Left:
KARRI TREE, WESTERN AUSTRALIA
Look up to the tops of the splendid karri trees and see how majestically they tower to the sky. One of the biggest trees in the world, and certainly the largest in Western Australia, the karri may take up to two centuries to reach its full height, after which only its girth will fatten. Rarely will it live for more than 500 years. Blossoming every four years and growing only in the south-west of the state where rainfall exceeds 1016 millimetres (40 ins) a year, the hard and heavy karri timber has proved to be exceptionally durable. Many tall trees can be seen along the scenic drives through forests preserved in national parks around Pemberton. This tree is one of the tallest, soaring to around seventy-five metres (265 feet).

Above:
ESPERANCE, WESTERN AUSTRALIA
Scattered along the coastline at Esperance there are many delightful sandy coves, sheltered by cliffs and bastions of chunky rocks. In the spring, wildflowers spread in glorious profusion over any slope that can hold enough soil for growth. Just out of the town there is a scenic drive that runs for ten kilometres through desolate but spectacular dunes. It follows the cliffs to Observatory Point, where the views are indeed lovely. It is a pleasant drive, for not only is the road excellent, but there are many side bays to pull into for viewing the inlets and sea with their incredible variations of blue. There is more superb coastal scenery at Cape Le Grand, about twenty-eight kilometres out of Esperance.

FORTESCUE RIVER, WESTERN AUSTRALIA

About twenty kilometres from Millstream there are some idyllic picnic and camping spots by the Fortescue River, which is shaded by magnificent stands of the paperbark melaleucas, river gums and palms. Shade is a rare and precious commodity in the northern areas of Australia and, after days of travelling over harsh plains where struggling trees give little, if any, shade from the burning midday sun, it is an exquisite relief to find a camp site like this one. During the winter months the Fortescue River is mostly dry, except for a number of pools which are fed by springs. It is believed that for about twelve kilometres the river runs underground, emerging at one of the deep shingle areas which is a characteristic of the river bed. Some parts of the river

are bordered by rich cliffs and, together with a few palms spilling like green fountains at their base, present a lovely picture when mirrored deeply in the water on a still evening. The palm that grows by the Fortescue River (*Livistona alfredii*) is found only in the vicinity of Millstream. There are a few date palms along the banks, too, planted by early squatters during the last century. Beside the neat Livistona, these palms seem quite untidy with their mass of side shoots sprouting everywhere. Fed by summer rains mostly borne on the tail-end of cyclones, the Fortescue River starts in the highland country to the south-east of the Hamersley Range and, after roaming the plains for about 640 kilometres, enters the Indian Ocean south-west of Roebourne.

MARBLE BAR, WESTERN AUSTRALIA

The town of Marble Bar, lying 183 kilometres inland from Port Hedland and 1530 kilometres from Perth, was named after this brilliantly-coloured mass of rock that crosses the Coongan River a few kilometres out of the town. Although parts of it look very much like marble, it is actually jasper, streaked with vivid colours of red, orange, white and grey-black. If the visitor can take the trouble to throw a bucket of water over a section of this fascinating striation, the bar will shine marvellously. Over the centuries the bar has been scratched and worn by debris sweeping down in floods, and the relentless abrasion still continues when the Coongan comes down. For most of the year the river is dry, with a small pool left here and there. But during the summer months, if the rains are good, it may flow two or three times in the season. Marble Bar's greatest claim to fame, however, is its climate. The town has the rather dubious distinction of being the hottest place in Australia. It's not just the temperature rising to abnormally high figures that gives it the reputation, but the consistent heat of the daily maximum often exceeding 37·8°C for weeks on end. Just the thought of their longest heatwave is enough to make any southerner melt—for 160 days in the summer of 1923/24 the temperature reached 37·8°C or higher. Yet the heat did not stop the gold prospectors of the 1880s, and for many years Marble Bar was a booming mining town.

Coastline

There is no doubt that Australians love their coastline and obtain maximum enjoyment from it. All the year round they flock to the seaboard for a multitude of sporting activities, but many desire only to enjoy the beautiful scenery. Access by road and walking track to many areas in the south and east of the country is relatively easy and there are often superb views from some of the major highways, especially Victoria's Great Ocean Road and north Queensland's Cook Highway.

However, in the north and west, the coast is still largely virgin ground, untouched and waiting to be explored. In the Kimberley region treacherous tides and innumerable reefs forbid access to most of the ragged and torn coast. Here, the off-shore waters are littered with a profusion of stony islands. The shores of Cape York and the Gulf of Carpentaria, forever bathed in heavy humidity, are fringed by jungles of mangroves that hold back vast mudflats patterned with rivers.

Of all the coastal areas the beaches are the most popular, with their sweeping stretches of unbroken sands, wide and free. No particular area can claim to have the best because there are so many magnificent ones around the entire coastline. But one that ranks with the finest and where freedom truly reigns supreme, is Broome's Cable Beach, in Western Australia. This beach of dreams stretches for twenty-two kilometres over fine, soft sand and has a width of about 200 metres from the dunes to the waterline. The surf is gentle and shark-free; and the wonderful colours of the sea change constantly.

In sharp contrast to the beaches are the numerous areas of precipitous cliffs that plunge deeply to turbulent seas. The long lines of high, perpendicular walls of rock edging the Great Australian Bight and Victoria's Port Campbell district are really magnificent. More often than not cliffs mark a treacherous part of the coastline and their spectacular beauty hides sagas of tragedy surrounding wrecked ships and loss of life. One can only guess at the number of vessels strewn around the coast—and at the amount of treasure heaped in graveyards of watery darkness. In south-western Victoria, the Port Campbell coastline is still regarded as one of the most perilous in the world for shipping.

In legends and stories of the Australian coast, whaling has always featured prominently. In those wild and adventurous days many of the southern towns were used as whaling bases long before settlements sprang up. Today there is only one base left on the mainland, and that is in the far south-west of Western Australia, at Frenchman's Bay, near Albany. It is a setting straight out of the whaling story books. Here the desolate coastline of massive boulders and craggy inlets is wild and forlorn. Even on stormy days, when the air is damp and the moaning wind stirs the seas to lash angrily at bleak headlands and small bays, the beauty is wildly wonderful.

All around Australia hundreds of islands skirt the shores. The majority are continental in origin, and once belonged to the mainland, but became separated by submergence or erosion. Many lie in clusters or in lonely isolation and vary in size from small outcrops of rocks, shallow mudflats and coral cays to mountainous masses of wild splendour. Many of them are very beautiful and have much charm, especially the ones off the Queensland coast. These lie like jewels in the sparkling blue water, their hilly slopes clothed in lovely forests and their shores dotted with sandy beaches lapped by calm seas. In winter, more and more southerners escape to these isles of paradise, for warmth and carefree days.

But the greatest treasure of the entire coastline is the Great Barrier Reef. It extends from the Torres Strait to just south of Gladstone and laces the many islands that lie in its path. This phenomenal stretch of coral, which harbours exotic marine life of great beauty, demands seeing, either through a glass-bottom boat, underwater observatory or, better still, by skindiving. Nowhere in the world are there coral reefs to compare with the Great Barrier Reef. Through countless ages, corals have been built up by polyps and, providing these tiny creatures are left unmolested, the coral will slowly grow into the miraculous formations that we see on the reef today.

Above:

FOWLERS BAY, SOUTH AUSTRALIA

Lying 130 kilometres east of the head of the Great Australian Bight, Fowlers Bay is bordered by magnificent white dunes sculptured by the wind into peaks, crevasses and cliffs. In places these are so vast that scenes resemble the Sahara Desert. The dunes are constantly on the move, and are slowly creeping towards the now abandoned Fowlers Bay village, the drifting sands swallowing fences and tracks, and eventually the buildings. Once visited frequently by whalers during the first half of the 19th Century, Fowlers Bay became a port in the 1890s for shipping wheat and other primary produce. In 1840 the explorer Edward John Eyre used the place as a depot for stores for his incredible journey along the coast to Western Australia. Now only fishermen come here.

Right:

POINT LABATT, SOUTH AUSTRALIA

Point Labatt, part of the coastline renowned for its spectacular cliffs, is situated about fifty kilometres south of Streaky Bay, on the west coast of the Eyre Peninsula. On a sandy beach at the bottom of the cliffs there is a permanent seal colony, though unfortunately the numbers are considerably fewer than in earlier years. There is a track down to the beach, but most people balk at the initial scramble over the cliff edge to reach the narrow ledge tucked under the cliff top from which the path starts. Once the main slope is reached, care must be taken as the ground is loose and crumbly. The seals appear to lead a life of utter bliss, with nothing better to do than lie around and snooze in the sun.

Top left:

KALBARRI, WESTERN AUSTRALIA

The rugged coastal gorges at Red Bluff terminate in splendid cliffs of coloured sandstone, and in places the surf can be heard thundering into the caves below. This national park lies 640 kilometres north of Perth.

Bottom left:

CABLE BEACH, WESTERN AUSTRALIA

This spacious beach, where overcrowding at any time is virtually impossible, lies a few kilometres out of Broome. Free from sharks, and ideal for swimming even when the tide is out, the vast sands are bordered by low dunes that vary in shades from white to red and that stretch for many kilometres. At one end lies Gantheaume Point, a craggy bluff of brilliant red rocks, famous for the dinosaur's footprint that lies embedded in a rock about thirty metres out to sea. It is only exposed at low king tides.

Above:

WILSONS PROMONTORY, VICTORIA

This part of the Promontory's coastline is near the lighthouse, which tops a steep hill scattered with many granite tors of incredible shapes and sizes. Situated in Gippsland, 240 kilometres south-east of Melbourne, Wilsons Promontory is the most southerly point of the Australian continent and juts deep into the waters of Bass Strait. It is one of the country's most exciting national parks for nature lovers. Here forest-clad mountains drop to the sea to meet the wide, sweeping beaches of the beautiful bays and coves that are tucked between the bold granite headlands. Clear sparkling streams, sheltered by lichened rocks and huge sprays of green ferns, flow merrily through the numerous deep gullies of the hills. Even the weather, which is often broodingly overcast or wild and stormy, adds beauty and character to 'The Prom', as it is lovingly called by Victorians. Access to most of the scenery is by walking track only.

Top left:

PORT MACQUARIE, NEW SOUTH WALES

Situated 370 kilometres north of Sydney, Port Macquarie has some picturesque stretches of coastline, studded with rocky bays and sandy inlets. The town stands close to the shore and is a popular place for vacationers.

Bottom left:

NAMBUCCA HEADS, NEW SOUTH WALES

Here the Nambucca River enters the sea, 517 kilometres north of Sydney. Nambucca Heads is a particularly delightful holiday resort; the coast is marked with magnificent beaches and pleasant spots lie along the Nambucca River. From various lookout points set high on the cliff tops, there are some lovely panoramas of the town, the coast, and the wide river spreading into still backwaters and lagoons just before it enters the sea.

Above:

TWELVE APOSTLES, VICTORIA

As the sun sinks low in the sky, the limestone cliffs turn hues of gold and brown, and the sea mist softens the craggy contours of the Twelve Apostles, lying in the Port Campbell National Park. These twelve monoliths rearing over the rolling surf are part of a treacherous piece of coast that has claimed fifty vessels and many lives, and is still feared by seafarers the world over. The national park covers about thirty-two kilometres of coastline, between Cape Otway and Warrnambool, in western Victoria. It offers some wonderfully grand scenery. Topped by plains, the cliffs drop vertically to the waterline. In many places, waves born out of wild and stormy seas have worn away sections of the cliff to archways, tunnels and gorges. Around Loch Ard there are some splendid formations, and here it is fascinating to watch the powerful swell heaving the sea up against the cliffs.

Above:

MALLACOOTA INLET, VICTORIA

It is not hard to find peace and contentment around this
beautiful inlet, where nature goes through an amazing repertoire
of changing moods that turn the picturesque waterways into
shimmering avenues of enchantment. The climate is mild all the
year round and the fishing is good, so it is with joy that people
come here to forget the hustle and bustle of cities. Lying in the far
eastern pocket of Gippsland, the lakes were formed by the silting
up of the Genoa River estuary, and many hectares of the land
edging the shoreline have been preserved as a national park. The
small town, whose population swells considerably in the holiday
season, is the base for fishermen harvesting Australia's richest
abalone beds.

Right:

COOLOOLA COLOURED SANDS, QUEENSLAND

These spectacular cliffs of sandstone line the Teewah Beach for
about thirty-two kilometres near Noosa Heads, north of
Brisbane. Rising to sixty-one metres (200 feet), they are relics of a
system of iron-stained dunes that were deposited many
thousands of years ago when the sea level was much lower. The
sand is covered with a fine crust that gives the appearance of
hardness, but in fact the dunes are quite fragile and will crumble
easily. Consequently, they are at the mercy of storms and
cyclones, and are slowly receding. The canyons, bluffs and hills
shaped in the sands are shaded in a bewildering variety of
colours; and a mass of white sand lying in a red canyon might
appear remarkably like a miniature glacier.

NEAR PORT DOUGLAS, QUEENSLAND

There is a wide variety of coastal scenery along the road that runs from Cairns to Port Douglas. Jungle-clad mountains fall dramatically to the sea, their lush tropical vegetation held back from the water by a narrow band of sand or a curved line of rocks. In many spots lovely bays and inlets give way to sandy flats exposed only at low tide. Here, like other places in northern Queensland, the sea goes out a long way at low tide, leaving uncovered the sturdy roots of mangroves that spread their roots in tangled patterns of twists and knots. Colonies of them cling to the shoreline and become a common sight as the coast pushes further north towards the tropics. They favour salt or brackish water, especially in muddy places where the water is relatively calm, and the mouth of subtropical and tropical rivers proves an ideal place for their growth. Although in many tropical countries the mangrove is valued as timber — mainly for firewood — very little is known about this strange, water-loving tree. The Australian Institute of Marine Science is conducting a series of studies into it along the Queensland coast. In the everglades of Hinchinbrook Island alone, over fifty species have been found. It is now known that the leaves are edible and contain about five times the amount of protein than that of the soya bean, and it seems that the mangrove is capable of turning large amounts of carbon dioxide into oxygen. Who knows?; in the future they may help combat pollution in cities!

WHITSUNDAY SUNSET, QUEENSLAND

Some of the loveliest islands of the Great Barrier Reef lie off Proserpine, in Whitsunday Passage, which has been acclaimed as 'one of the world's most beautiful waterways. Extending for about thirty-two kilometres along the coast and in some places less than three kilometres wide, this rich stretch of water is flanked by many wooded islands of all sizes, lying like green gems in the sparkling sea. The vegetation is subtropical and many of the picturesque bays and inlets, with their sandy beaches, are lined by graceful native hoop pines, similar to the Norfolk pine. Most of the settled islands have a delightful network of walking tracks. These usually wind up to peaks or ridges where magnificent panoramas of the passage can be seen. Holiday resorts by palm-fringed beaches have been established on Hayman, Brampton, Daydream, South Molle, Long and Lindeman Islands. All offer the entertainments one would expect in a tropical playground. Visits to the outer Barrier Reef, which lies about eighty kilometres due east of the Whitsunday Islands, can only be made when the weather is stable and at low tide. The best time is when the tides are extremely low at full and new moon. The boats anchor just off the deep shelves of richly coloured coral. Then dinghies take the visitors to the exposed reef where they can fossick around the coral beds or snorkel in the lagoons to see something of the fascinating marine life visible only at low tide.

79

Top left:

HINCHINBROOK ISLAND, QUEENSLAND

This large and beautiful island of rugged mountains, peaks and superb beaches lies off the coast between Ingham and Cardwell. Navigation is tricky in the maze of waterways that lace the vast area of mangrove swamps in Missionary Bay. Nine broad rivers enter this bay from the swamps; further in there are another fifteen rivers; and after that, the number becomes improbable to count. All are thickly lined with mangroves and provide a haven for crocodiles.

Bottom left:

BARRIER REEF MARINE LIFE, QUEENSLAND

Many brightly-coloured fish and exotic marine creatures inhabit the fabulous coral reef which extends 2000 kilometres down the north-eastern coast of Australia.

Above:

CAPE LE GRAND, WESTERN AUSTRALIA

Lying east of Esperance on the southern seaboard of the state and facing the Recherche Archipelago, this national park has some splendid coastal scenery. Headlands walled in granite are thrust into the brilliantly-coloured sea, and stony peaks are frequently veiled in sea mist. Unbelievably-white sand lines the gently-curving bays. It is so fine that it squeaks underfoot and, when pressed in the hand, feels like talc powder. Oddly-shaped rocks sometimes coated in red lichen litter the coastal slopes, as if carelessly flung down by a great hand. One tall monolith at Thistle Cove is called the Whistling Rock, because when the wind blows in a certain direction the rock seems to emit from its core a shrieking howl—a sound weird and ghostly to all who hear it.

Tasmania

Tasmanians have every right to claim their State is the most beautiful in Australia. This heart-shaped island, lying about 240 kilometres off the south-eastern corner of the continent, has an overwhelming amount of beautiful scenery in an area less than a third the size of Victoria. Unlike the mainland, distances between beauty spots are negligible.

The finest alpine country lies in the far south-west and in the central highlands around Cradle Mountain and Lake St Clair, where wild and rugged mountains of serrated ridges and sharp peaks are often shrouded in polar-born snow and mist. Roads now go to Dove Lake at the foot of Cradle Mountain and, in the south-west, to the new and vast Lake Pedder where the splendid landscapes resemble New Zealand or Norway. However, Lake Pedder's beauty was gained by losing a priceless treasure, for the original lake, famed for its unique beach and accessible only by walking track, was flooded when the Gordon River Power Development Scheme built its storage dams. Conservationists around the globe were appalled at the loss, but the lake did not stand a chance against progress. However, one positive result is that now thousands of people can enjoy its beauty instead of only a few. Unfortunately there are many raw wounds around the dam sites where construction machinery brutally ravaged the earth and it will take many years before the bare hillsides will be covered again with vegetation. Yet the transcendent loveliness of the lake, when it becomes a gigantic mirror reflecting the clouds and majestic mountains, is undeniable.

Much of Tasmania's scenery and celebrated landforms are associated with the island's early history, which in terms of European settlement is the second oldest after New South Wales. One historic town with a rather startling feature is Stanley, where the buildings cluster around the base of a table-topped headland known as the Nut. Rising dramatically to 137 metres (450 feet) at the end of an isthmus off the far north-west coast, the Nut was originally known as Circular Head, and its pioneer settlement became the administration centre for the Van Diemen's Land Company. Today Stanley is a quaint little fishing village full of links with the past. Some of the best views of the Nut are from the road that winds past the once-magnificent Highfield Estate. For fine panoramas of the north-west coast, take a walk up the well-made, though steep, path to the top of the Nut. Covered with tussocky grass, its plateau of about thirty hectares is surprisingly undulating and, although windswept and desolate, a colony of mutton birds still finds it a good home; their burrows are visible at the far end.

An area in south-east Tasmania rich in both scenery and history is the Tasman Peninsula. This irregular and indented piece of land is the southern part of two peninsulas joined by a narrow isthmus only eighteen metres wide. This is known as Eaglehawk Neck, and one of the reasons for establishing the young colony's early, grim prison at Port Arthur was that the isthmus presented a natural 'gate' that was relatively easy to guard. Today the remains of the penitentiary lie peacefully in picturesque parkland and are visited by thousands of tourists each year. As well as these famous ruins, there are many wonderful landforms—the Tasman Arch, Tessellated Pavement, Devil's Kitchen, caves and blowholes—lying along the peninsula's scenic coast of spectacular cliffs and tranquil bays. At the far southern capes, columns of dolerite lie in the cliffs like splendid organ pipes.

Another beautiful place that once held a penitentiary and is now a major tourist attraction is Maria Island, lying off Orford and Triabunna on the east coast. The northern part is the most spectacular with its central rugged ridge; a scenic feature is the Painted Cliffs, two kilometres from the small settlement of Darlington. Here relentless weathering by wind and waves has fashioned extraordinary patterns in the sandstone to resemble a honeycomb filled with whorls of chocolate and cream. Declared a national park in 1971, the island is responsible for preserving the numerous historical buildings of the penal settlement as well as the scenery and wildlife. Perhaps the most heart-warming job the park has is to provide safe breeding grounds for two species of animals and birds now facing extinction in Tasmania—the Forester kangaroo and the Cape Barren goose. The gulls roost quietly on the beach and the Cape Barren Geese confidently strut about the place, honking like contented pigs.

CRADLE MOUNTAIN, TASMANIA

Situated in the central Tasmanian highlands, eighty kilometres from Devonport, this magnificent mountain of serrated ridge-tops and thrusting, jagged peaks soars to around 1500 metres (5000 feet). It lies at the end of Dove Lake. The lake's basin, gouged deeply by glacial actions millions of years ago, has a number of small, picturesque beaches covered with coarse, white sand around its edge. This one, with the old Waldheim boatshed, is only about five minutes walk from the car park. Clear sunny days are not common in this spectacular mountain region; if a day begins with promise, it is quite likely that after a few hours clouds heralding in bad weather will slip over the ranges. In an amazingly short time, heavy curtains of mist and

rain will sweep over the land, obliterating everything for days, sometimes weeks. Covering an area of 1358 square kilometres, Cradle Mountain is part of a national park that extends to Lake St Clair eighty kilometres to the south. The park is linked by the famous hiking route, the Overland Track. This track is well defined and alpine huts are spaced between a day's walking and, even though it can be done in four days, most people take longer to explore the many interesting sidetracks. The greatest hazard of all walks taken in the park is the weather because, even in summer, snow and severe storms can suddenly envelop the land. It is essential that even day walkers register their route with the rangers.

DOVE AND WILKS LAKES, TASMANIA

From the Face Track on Cradle Mountain there are wonderful views of these lakes. The smaller one, Lake Wilks, looks quite different from the ground level views, where the picturesque tarn, set high on the mountain slope, appears to balance precariously at the edge of the hillside. The golden vegetation colouring the slopes is the unique fagus (*Nothofagus gunii*), the only one of several deciduous trees endemic to Australia that have a spectacular display of autumn tints. Over a brief period at the end of April the tiny leaves change through shades of yellow and orange to bronze and, when they fall, the ground seems to be covered in shavings of burnished copper and gold. When the fagus is in its golden glory, the best walk to take is through the

Ballroom Forest to Lake Wilks, returning via Marion's Lookout. An exciting walk at any time is from the Face Track to the summit of the mountain. This walk is much easier than it seems from below and no climbing equipment is needed. Near the summit the defined path disappears into a tangled mass of boulders that get bigger and more grotesque as the top is approached, but are easy enough to scramble over. The route is marked by red splashes of paint on the rocks. Just when the hiker thinks he is at the top he is confronted with several astonishing valleys of massive tumbled tors surrounded by monstrous columns of rock; from this incredible Stonehenge-like world, so grey and stark, the views are breathtaking.

Left:
RUSSELL FALLS, TASMANIA
Situated on the lower slopes of Mount Field, eighty-three kilometres north-west of Hobart, this lovely waterfall is at its best in spring when the river is swollen from seasonal rains and melting snows. At this time the water spills over the tiers with tremendous force, creating a strong breeze that fans mist into every nook and cranny around the falls. Nearly as spectacular as the falls is the canopy of huge, and very old, Man Ferns (*Dicksonia antarctica*) that line the end section of the walking path. In the coolness and dampness of the shade, lichens and lush green mosses are draped over every rock, fallen branch and fern trunk, reluctantly giving space to an assortment of dank and dreary fungi. The walk to the falls is only ten minutes away from the car park and the well-defined path follows the Russell Falls River.

Above:
LAKE PEDDER, TASMANIA
From the top of Red Knoll Lookout, at the end of Scotts Peak Road, Lake Pedder's splendid beauty is shrouded in a mist, which lies like a sea of soft fleece and increases in brilliance as the sun moves high in the sky. Generally the mist will lift quite suddenly, leaving behind gossamer shreds of cloud that lazily wait to be chased away by a playful breeze. Lake Pedder is at Strathgordon, 170 kilometres from Hobart.

Overpage:
LAKE PEDDER, NEAR SCOTTS PEAK DAM
The beauty of the new Lake Pedder is wonderful and the scenic roads around the lake are now open to the public. Part of the Gordon River Development Scheme, the lake is joined by a channel to Lake Gordon; together they hold the largest quantity of water in Australia.

NEAR EAGLEHAWK NECK, TASMANIA

The Tasman Peninsula, linked by a thread of land only eighteen metres wide to the Forestier Peninsula at Eaglehawk Neck, has a splendid variety of coastal scenery. Tree-lined coves and inlets—their sandy shores lapped by gentle waves—lie in shelter from the turbulent ocean. Massive dunes give way to sheer and craggy cliffs skirted by wide aprons of rock where waves relentlessly spill foaming seawater. There are some strange and wonderful landforms in this region—the grand Tasman Arch, the formidable Devils Kitchen and, near Port Arthur, the Remarkable Cave which has a large and eerie tunnel leading out to the tumultuous surf. Lying near Eaglehawk Neck, the Blowhole gives

good entertainment. The arrival of each wave is announced by a thunderous roar as it rushes along the narrow corridor of rock before exploding out the end. A more relaxing coastal feature of interest, and one that can be explored in relative safety, is the Tessellated Pavement, also at Eaglehawk Neck. The pavement is a geological curiosity and demonstrates nature's teasing ways, for this extensive area of flat rock seems to have been worked diligently by a stone mason. Earth movements fractured the rocks in such a way that it appears tiled, and waves carrying sand and gravel helped smooth out the area. Some of the tiles have shallow basins, formed by a chemical action with sea water.

DERWENT VALLEY, TASMANIA

After the untamed and wild mountains, which are less than an hour's drive from here, the landscapes of the valley appear extraordinarily soft and peaceful. The neatness of the trees, orchards and hop farms is more in keeping with rural England than Australia. Winding its way through the valley, the wide and beautiful Derwent River is one of the island's major arteries. It rises in Lake St Clair and, after travelling 193 kilometres, the river enters the sea downstream from the city of Hobart. Australia's supply of hops comes largely from Tasmania, much of it grown on the rich, alluvial flats by the Derwent River. Wherever there are hop farms, there are rows of stately, splendid poplars, for these trees provide the necessary wind break for the hops which must be supported on high wires. Come autumn, with so many poplar trees and English willows lining the river and creeks, the valley is ablaze in gold. During this season the hedges of Hawthorn and Rosehips bordering roads and lanes are covered in a profusion of red berries. In early autumn, many of the trees in the orchards are laden with lush fruit, ready for harvesting. It is a tranquil valley and, except for the hustle and bustle of harvest time, life appears as sedate as the Derwent River itself.

Top left:

THE NUT, TASMANIA

This table-topped headland called the Nut rises at the end of an isthmus and shelters the small fishing village of Stanley, on the north-west coast. In the town there are many interesting historic buildings which are being carefully preserved by the townsfolk.

Bottom left:

GUNNS PLAINS, TASMANIA

This rural area of rich soil lies in a spacious, lush green valley sheltered by towering mountains south of Penguin, on the north-west coast. The valley always seems to be green and is best approached from the steep road leading in from Riana. The district has quantities of high-grade limestone and, as typical of limestone country, there are caves full of beautiful formations, some of which have been illuminated for the public.

Above:

GREAT LAKE, TASMANIA

Like many of Tasmania's lakes, the Great Lake seems shy in revealing her beauty early in the morning, as wispy clouds of mist linger over the water after the initial fog disappears. Situated on the central plateau five kilometres from the edge of the Western Tiers escarpment and 1034 metres (3388 feet) above sea level, this lake was originally a series of smaller lakes which were flooded in 1922 when the dam at Miena was built. Until the enlargement of Lake Pedder, the Great Lake was the largest in Tasmania. From this point a tunnel carries water through the Western Tiers to the Poatina Power Station. The lake covers an area of about 170 square kilometres and provides wonderful fishing as trout were introduced as far back as 1864. At Breona, lying by the northern end of the lake, holiday shacks are grouped along the banks.

Above:

COLES BAY, TASMANIA

Lying midway on the east coast, 198 kilometres from Hobart, the bay and the holiday resort of Coles Bay are sheltered by towering guardians of red granite, known as the Hazards. These mountains were named after Captain Hazard, whose ship the *Promise* was wrecked in the bay last century. The little town lies at the edge of the Freycinet National Park, at the end of the slender finger of land that juts into the Tasman Sea. It was declared a national park as far back as 1916, and with Mount Field, is the oldest park in the State. There is some magnificent scenery in Freycinet, and one of the loveliest panoramas is Wineglass Bay. This is seen from the saddle between Mount Mayson and Mount Amos of the Hazards.

Right:

RICHMOND BRIDGE, TASMANIA

Built of freestone by convict labour in the period 1823 to 1825, this picturesque bridge spans the Coal River at Richmond and is the oldest in Australia. Legend has it that the bridge is haunted by the ghost of a cruel and unscrupulous overseer, who, during the construction, was flung by the angry convicts on to the rocks beneath the bridge. Through one of the six splendid arches can be seen the spire of St John's, the oldest Roman Catholic church in the country, built in 1835. Lying twenty-two kilometres from Hobart, Richmond is one of Tasmania's oldest towns; many of its historic buildings of beautiful stone laced with iron work have changed little over the past 100 years. One of the most formidable memorials of the convict days is the old gaol, now open to the public for inspection.

NEAR SCOTTSDALE, TASMANIA
The lovely undulating hills surrounding the town of Scottsdale in the north-east of the island were once covered by dense forest and, although much of it has been cleared for farming, there are still some pockets of lush vegetation left. Lying in the centre of a particularly rich belt of soil, the district has become well known for its growing of hops and flowers and, in the spring through to autumn, the countryside is full of beauty. Twenty kilometres to the north on the coast is the delightful village of Bridport, which, like so many of Tasmania's coastal settlements, offers excellent fishing and superb beaches.